100%
UNOFFICIAL

First published in Great Britain 2021 by 100% Unofficial,
a part of Farshore

An imprint of HarperCollins*Publishers*
1 London Bridge Street, London SE1 9GF
www.farshore.co.uk

HarperCollins*Publishers*
1st Floor, Watermarque Building, Ringsend Road
Dublin 4, Ireland

Written by Daniel Lipscombe
Edited by Craig Jelley
Designed by Anthony Duke
Illustrations by Matt Burgess
Cover Designed by John Stuckey

This book is an original creation by Farshore
© 2021 Farshore

ISBN 978 0 7555 0349 0
Printed in Romania
001

ONLINE SAFETY FOR YOUNGER FANS

Spending time online is great fun! Here are a few simple rules to help younger
fans stay safe and keep the internet a great place to spend time.

- Never give out your real name – don't use it as your username.
- Never give out any of your personal details.
- Never tell anybody which school you go to or how old you are.
- Never tell anybody your password, except a parent or guardian.
- Be aware that you must be 13 or over to create an account on many sites. Always check
the site policy and ask a parent or guardian for permission before registering.
- Always tell a parent or guardian if something is worrying you.

Stay safe online. Any website addresses listed in this book are correct at the
time of going to print. However, Farshore is not responsible for content hosted by
third parties. Please be aware that online content can be subject to change and
websites can contain content that is unsuitable for children. We advise that
all children are supervised when using the internet.

MIX
Paper from
responsible sources

FSC
www.fsc.org
FSC™ C007454

100% UNOFFICIAL

FORTNITE
ANNUAL 2022

CONTENTS

100% UNOFFICIAL

WELCOME TO THE FORTNITE ISLAND

As Fortnite celebrates its fourth year and gets ready for a fifth in 2022, take a minute to stand back and marvel at this titanic title. When Fortnite Battle Royale landed in 2017, no-one could have expected it to dominate the gaming world like it has. With over 250 million players, billions of hours of gaming time and a whole culture around it, the impact it made was extraordinary.

The Fortnite phenomenon continues at a powerful pace. Chapter 2 pulls out new surprises all the time, from bounties, gold bars, quests and Characters to cars, motorboats, secret agents and shakedowns. The island remains fresh and ever-changing, with new locations and points of interest springing up each season. And if that's not enough, jump into Party Royale for fun minigames, movies, shows and more!

In this epic independent and unofficial 2022 annual, you'll discover everything a Fortnite fanatic needs to know. Weapons, skins, locations, vehicles and top tactics are packed in to give you all the expert island info. So, get ready to join the Battle Bus and drop in for an awesome adventure!

CHAPTER 2: DEBRIEF

It's hard to imagine the Fortnite island without swimming, fishing, driving cool cars and taking on NPCs (non-playable characters). Chapter 2 has delivered these fan favourites and even more awesome additions to enjoy.

CROWD CONTROL

The introduction of NPCs in Chapter 2 added a new dimension to the game. Also called AIs, meaning artificial intelligence, these folk are dotted around the map to give players a special target to take out. Henchmen and marauders are types of NPCs that many of you will have battled with.

WATER WATCH

Back in Season X, diving into the water, splashing through lakes and speeding along on a motorboat was the stuff of dreams. Chapter 2 gave us all of these, along with the ability to fish for creatures like floppers and slurpfish (great for healing) and even plucking weapons and ammo from the water.

UP YOUR GAME

The upgrade bench appeared in the very first season of Chapter 2 and allowed you to trade materials to boost your weapon's power. It was a divisive element of the game that many players disliked and actively avoided, so Epic decided to restore order and it was vaulted in Season 5, although the upgrading principle remained with a new twist (see pages 12-13 for more info).

ISLAND INTRIGUE

Following the eye-popping Season X events of The End and Black Hole, Chapter 2 introduced an all-new island, packed with places and features never experienced before. The map took on a new identity through the seasons, changing from a flood zone to vast desert surrounding the Zero Point.

EXPECT THE UNEXPECTED ...

Chapter 2 has taught us that Epic Games, the developer, is not frightened to flip Fortnite upside down, shaking the game to create pulsating new themes and styles. Anything is possible, so bring your A-game every time you drop!

CHAPTER 2: DEBRIEF

FAMOUS FACES

Chapter 2 has been stuffed with tie-ins with famous movies, shows and superheroes, from Star Wars' Mandalorian to Marvel's Deadpool and Galactus, plus the deadly Gaming Legend Series featuring Master Chief and Kratos. It is HUGELY popular with the audience, and the big names and characters are always appearing in the world's biggest battle game.

FORTNITE CREW

Described as the 'ultimate subscription offer' by Epic, Fortnite Crew landed in Season 5 with a triple bonus for gamers who splash out on the service each month. Included is access to the current Battle Pass, 1,000 V-Bucks each month and an exclusive Crew Pack, which features a new skin, pickaxe and back bling. You can still play for free though!

CARS

Fortnite fans quickly revved up their consoles and PCs to get involved with the game's first driveable cars in Chapter 2. The chapter launched with four vehicle options and meant your squad could go for a ride together in much more style than an All Terrain Kart ever offered. Just be careful not to run out of fuel! Flick to pages 36-37 for more car-razy info.

LOOT SHARK

With all the water that flooded in during Season 3 of Chapter 2, it was perhaps no surprise that a new water-based transport arrived. Loot sharks are rideable creatures that pull you through the wet stuff at speed, leaping and lashing around in menacing moves. Just cast a fishing rod at a shark, wait for it to take the bait and you'll be off in its wild wake.

TIP

If you're desperate for a shark ride, prioritise picking up a fishing rod from nearby chests. Without one, you have no chance of snagging the big monster.

GAME-CHANGER: CHARACTERS

In Season 5, a cool NPC type, called Characters, appeared on the map. Over 40 of them can be found around the island, including old faves like Splode and Doggo. These automated players are marked by a speech bubble and there are several things you can receive from them.

BOUNTY

Accepting the Character's challenge of eliminating a specific opponent means you're taking on a bounty. Use the image and location instructions given to track down the opponent, then it's time to wipe them out of the game. Do this and you'll be given a special golden reward. Watch out, as there may also be a bounty on your head, making you the hunted target!

BOUNTY
Eliminate Enemy Player

REWARD 150

UPGRADE

Some Characters act as vendors, rather than hunters, and allow you to upgrade your weapons, giving you an advantage over your enemies. There are not many of these Character types around, and of course you need to pay them in gold bars for the service.

One man's wreck is this girl's pile of potential.

RARE > EPIC

UPGRADE 1,145 / 145

BARS

Complete a bounty and pocket some shiny gold bars, which are new to Chapter 2. Bars are a type of currency, separate and different to V-Bucks, which can be used to get a high-level weapon, upgrade inventory items and even hire a Character to fight alongside you. Don't forget to 'chat' with a Character to see what they offer in exchange for bars.

GAME-CHANGER: CHARACTERS

TIP

Gold bars can't be bought with real life money or V-Bucks, so get collecting and earning them so that you can trade with the Characters.

FINDING BARS

As well as being earned through bounties, gold bars also pop up around the new-look Season 5 map. Open safes to capture a clutch of these glittering beauties and watch out for them being dropped by eliminated opponents too. Your level of bars appears onscreen, alongside your mats, and remember that they carry over – no need to spend them all in one match.

QUESTS

Quests reward players with gold bars as well. Check out what a Character wants you to do in order to complete their quest and collect some gold from it as your treat. Other quests are set as daily or weekly challenges, giving a player XP rewards. In Season 5, these types of quests were rated in one of five rarities – common to legendary – for the first time.

Something jumped on my car and made us swerve into a ditch! When I got out... it vanished.

QUEST
Catch air in a Vehicle

REWARD   60

INTEL

Characters will also help a player by providing intel (intelligence) on their map surroundings, offering assistance which may get them deeper into the game. Sometimes, though, you may just be in the mood for a fight and fancy challenging a Character to a duel. Imagine taking on Brutus, reveling in that mighty victory and picking up a sweet weapon in return! Take the challenge if you dare.

EXOTIC WEAPONS

If the five usual rarities of weapons, plus the mythic type, aren't enough for you, how about a super seventh version instead? Exotic weapons became a part of the game in Chapter 2, but at a heavy cost of well over a thousand gold bars. Each of them are only available through a purchase from a Character. Storm scout rifle, the dub, boom sniper rifle, the big chill and the impressive night hawk with thermal scope were among the first batch of exotic firearms that players could barter for with Characters.

BACK TO BASICS

It never hurts to go over the essentials of playing Fortnite – we could all use a reminder now and again. These pages will show you everything you need to know to polish your basic skills and give yourself a good foundation to your game.

DROPPING IN

In the main Battle Royale mode, up to 99 other players will drop from the flying Battle Bus onto the island. Act quickly as you'll need to gather weapons and resources to progress and beat the enemies around you.

☐ Gather the essential materials (mats) of wood, stone and metal.

☐ Pick up weapons from chests or eliminated players.

☐ Stay within the storm's shrinking safe zone, protecting your health and shield to be the last player standing.

BUILDING

While winning without having to build is possible, it's pretty much vital that you build some structures in a tense battle situation. Building gives you protection, can bridge you between locations and even trap the enemy.

- [ ] Know how to build a wooden ramp quickly, for better sniping spots and spying positions.

- [ ] Wooden and brick walls and fences can give near-instant cover from attack fire.

- [ ] Being able to edit fast and alter a building, by perhaps adding a door or window, is a mega skill too.

WEAPONS

There have been hundreds of types, rarities and ammo options for weapons in Battle Royale. Knowing your way around a shotgun, rifle or machine gun can be the difference between early elimination and reaching the endgame.

- [ ] In simple terms, the higher grade the weapon, the better it is. In Chapter 2, levels went from common to exotic.

- [ ] SMGs suit close-quarter fights, sniper rifles are for destruction at distance and assault rifles are great all-rounders.

- [ ] Explosives like grenades and rocket launchers can cause chaos and confusion for solo players and squads.

THE MAP

Chapter 2 brought with it plenty of game-changing map alterations. Let's take a look at the lay of the latest landscape.

LOW POINT

After the floods of Season 3, the waters receded in later seasons and more land mass returned. The north-west's Coral Castle sprung up, sitting at a low sea level and open to attack from higher ground around.

VIKING VICTORY

The Viking ship close to Holly Hedges, and its surrounding area, is a reliable source of goodies in the early game. Chapter 2 of Season 5 also introduced the Ragnarok Character here, where there's the chance to grab his epic compact SMG (P90) if he's defeated after a duel.

SWAMPED IN

Slurpy Swamp has been through a few changes in Chapter 2, but it remains the healing place-to-be, owing to the reviving slurp water inside it. Some players enjoy landing here to get an early-game boost. The Flushed Building landmark arrived in Season 5.

STEALTHY STRONGHOLD

CORAL CASTLE

PLEASANT PAR

SWEATY SANDS

SALTY TOWERS

HOLLY HEDGES

WEEPING WOODS

SLURPY SWAMP

Map labels:

CRAGGY CLIFFS

STEAMY STACKS

COLOSSAL COLISEUM

DIRTY DOCKS

TER'S HAVEN

RETAIL ROW

LAZY LAKE

CATTY CORNER

MISTY MEADOWS

DESERT

A desert biome appeared way back in Season 5 of Chapter 1, covering a large stretch in the south-west. Again in Season 5 of Chapter 2, the dusty stuff returned around the new Zero Point central spot.

DOCK DROP

The most easterly named location, Dirty Docks appeared at the very start of Chapter 2 and remains popular throughout the seasons. As other new places and POIs attract curious players, making a drop here still rewards you with plenty of loots and spawns around the mass of buildings.

FELINE GREAT

The general area around Catty Corner became a bit of a no-go, or no interest, zone for many from Season 3 onwards. But there are still spots to loot, including the gas station and factory, before heading towards nearby Lazy Lake and Retail Row.

NAME GAME

What do you know about the new locations, familiar (and unfamiliar) points of interest and the places to drop and play in Chapter 2? Read on for a revealing round up of the island's hottest spots!

ZERO POINT

With the Zero Point's dramatic return in Season 5, after disappearing at the end of Chapter 1, a large desert zone was also created around it. Hogging the centre of the island, Zero Point is not for the weak (watch out for sinking sand!) although there are many loot chests and rewards to claim. Epic actually hailed this as the Zero Point season – find out more about the Zero Point Crystals on page 38.

SALTY TOWERS

If you were a fan of Tilted Towers (who wasn't?) then this classic new zone was perfect for you when it was created in Season 5. Merged with Salty Springs, the place is littered with sand as it's right next to the desert biome. Use the high rise opportunities as a way to get on top of the opposition.

COLOSSAL COLISEUM

If you're feeling brave and have stocked up with your favourite legendary weapons, then you might fancy your chances in a gladiatorial battle within this historical arena. It's a place that can change each time you visit, as objects appear there at random. It can be tough to escape if you find yourself outnumbered or outgunned because of the enforced walls and steep stairs. Keep an eye out, and not just for the gold Peely statues, or you'll end up dying a gladiator's death!

STEALTHY STRONGHOLD

Welcome to the jungle! Towards the far north-east corner of the island sits the Stealthy Stronghold, which is a large, densely wooded area penned in by a concrete wall. Occupying the spot where Homely Hills was, Stealthy Stronghold contains a decent dose of rewards, with plenty of clearings and covered spots to hunt down targets too.

HUNTER'S HAVEN

Wedged between Lazy Lake and Weeping Woods, just south of the central desert, Hunter's Haven became home to several buildings with loot potential when it popped up in Chapter 2. Use these hideouts to pick off opponents in the open and track down the Lexa Character, who is fiercely protected by Imagined Order (IO) Guards.

PLEASANT PARK

After a stint in Stealthy Stronghold with your squad, venture south to explore the much more laid-back Pleasant Park. It made its return to the map in Season 5, replacing Doom's Domain, and you'll be greeted by many familiar sights of suburban houses and even a football pitch ... perfect for a shootout with your pals. Lots of early Season 5 quests sent players to this formerly favourite area so they could refamiliarise themselves with it. Ever since, it's become a popular location, with plenty of loot available in the many lofts and basements.

NAME GAME

BUTTER BARN

This is not a large landmark, but gamers get a good buzz from rocking up at this ranch-style location north of Hunter's Haven. For starters, the Mancake Character hangs out here and the night hawk exotic scoped revolver can be picked up from him in exchange for gold bars. Jump in a nearby motorboat and move swiftly to Colossal Coliseum or Salty Towers in the desert biome.

THE DURR BURGER

Located south of Holly Hedges and west of Weeping Woods, the Durrr Burger restaurant landmark returned in Chapter 2 of Season 5 in the spot where Logjam Woodworks stood. With a long history in Fortnite, starting out in Greasy Grove, the eatery boasts as many as six chests and is home to Beef Boss Character.

THE PIZZA PIT

Head north-east from the Durrr Burger, taking a sandy track through the desert, and you'll reach this rival franchise serving another fave Fortnite food. The remains of the original restaurant from Tomato Town are here, although almost completely covered in sand, and the remnants of the Pass N Gas station are also nearby. Scope it out for loot and a meeting with the Tomato Head NPC to see what tasty treats he has to offer wayward visitors.

CRAGGY CLIFFS

First appearing in Chapter 2, Season 1, Craggy Cliffs featured on the Battle Royale map for many seasons, even though it went through severe floods and was once in the grip of Ghost and Shadow Henchman. In Season 5, the Fishstick NPC took up residence here and Remedy could be found nearby too, offering helpful healing rewards.

LAZY LAKES

Because of its position in the south-east central zone, its large scale and abundance of loot and chests, Lazy Lakes remains a hot drop spot through Chapter 2. Confident players are ready to accept an early game duel here and mop up the weapons on offer, then perhaps head west for a battle in Hunter's Haven.

WHICH WEAPON?

Chapter 2 has been packed with an awesome array of firearms, some new to the game and others with a classic vibe. Take a look at some of the very best weapons to have at your fingertips.

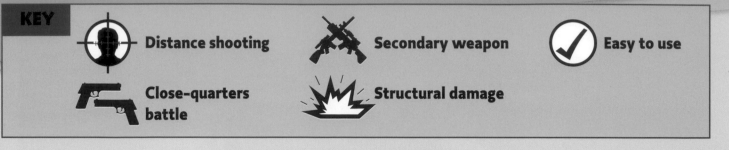

KEY

- ⊕ **Distance shooting**
- 🔫 **Close-quarters battle**
- ⚔ **Secondary weapon**
- 💥 **Structural damage**
- ✓ **Easy to use**

THE DUB

Introduced as part of the cool new exotic variant of weapons in Chapter 2, the dub has the same stats as the legendary double barrel shotgun. It looks and sounds fierce, with a familiar feel that makes you appear like an old skool fighter.

Best For:

Best For: ⊕

BOOM SNIPER RIFLE

Another exciting exotic weapon, the boom sniper cost a mighty 1,225 gold bars in Season 5, but for many it was a price worth paying. Firing an explosive clinger from mid to long range, it also has a mag size of five, compared to just one for the heavy sniper rifle it is based on.

Best For:

DRAGON'S BREATH SHOTGUN

Need a red-hot firearm? Pick up this piece, available as an epic or legendary, which first appeared in Chapter 2, Season 5. Your opponents will burst into flames as soon as they're hit by a bullet. Structures can be set on fire as well, but you'll need to get up close for the full fiery effect from this potentially catastrophic weapon.

LEVER ACTION RIFLE

If you can get over the extended reload time - up to six seconds! - this lengthy weapon is a real star for picking people off from afar. There's no adjustable scope to make it useful at closer ranges, but it does have an increased zoom. Some pros have even been known to use it as an emergency stand-in for an assault rifle, though it won't have anything like the rapid output of an AR.

Best For:

25

WHICH WEAPON?

SCAR ASSAULT RIFLE

Best For:

Let's not beat about the bush – the epic and legendary versions of the assault rifle have been a Fortnite fave for years! Known as the SCAR it uses medium bullets and can hold up to 30 in the magazine. It's an all-round star on the battle ground and great at any range. Crouch down and pop away – the scar won't let you down.

THE BIG CHILL

Best For:

Remember this wacky 'weapon' from Season 5? It deals zero damage and DPS, instead hitting a player's mobility and making them slip and slide around while you and your squad hopefully take advantage. It's similar to the equally-fun chiller grenade.

Best For:

PISTOL

The epic and legendary pistol reappeared in Season 5 of Chapter 2, replacing the very similar revolver handgun, and as a close-range or back-up gun it is more than worthy of the job. In purple and orange flavours, the pistol can reach nearly 200 DPS, so an accurate headshot is a mighty useful accomplishment. They can be tricky to master though, especially for those who are used to an AR or SMG.

SUBMACHINE GUN

Known as an SMG, this rapid-fire beauty has a habit of switching between being vaulted and unvaulted. When it's in play, use the SMG's high DPS and hit rate to blast the enemy at short distance. Structures, too, can take a beating from it. Its scattershot firing pattern means you can use from the hip and not be shy with the trigger!

Best For:

TIP

With the SMG, always keep a close eye on your ammo level. It rips through its light bullets in no time and you don't want to be left holding an unloaded weapon.

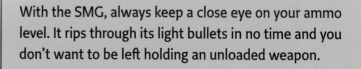

WHICH WEAPON?

TIP

The night hawk is useful if you need to use a weapon in the storm because the thermal view finder boosts your vision through the haze.

NIGHT HAWK

Best For:

Basically it's the scoped revolver but in the fancy new exotic variant, and gamers went a little crazy when they got their fingers on this firearm for the first time. With decent damage numbers for a small piece, its thermal scope is a helpful tool to home in on targets. A very cool name, too!

Best For:

AMBAN SNIPER RIFLE

A rifle that also does damage as a melee weapon? That's exactly what the amban sniper rifle is. Appearing in Chapter 2, Season 5, and yours if you defeated the Mandalorian, it deals high level damage to buildings and unsuspecting opponents from a great range. It has thermal vision and can also be used like a spear in combat.

Best For:

SHADOW TRACKER

With a red and white finish, the shadow tracker looks special and has a unique function to match. It's most similar to the suppressed pistol, but its party trick is that it can mark the opponent it strikes and keep them highlighted for a short while. It's difficult to hide after being tagged by this clever piece of kit.

ROCKET LAUNCHER

Thankfully, the powerful rocket launcher was unvaulted in Season 5 of Chapter 2 and could be obtained by eliminating the Ruckus NPC. As one of the most fun weapons ever to hit the island, it's a total riot from distance and can wreak absolute havoc on buildings and structures, often causing fall damage if you can't manage a direct hit.

Best For:

CHAPTER 2 SKINS

What has been your favourite outfit from Chapter 2? Flick through some of the best skins and looks from recent seasons.

AGENT PEELY

Available in ghost, shadow and golden agent styles, Agent Peely is still eye-catching now after being released in Season 2 of Chapter 2. It's a spy-flavoured variation of the popular Peely skin, which first appeared in Chapter 1.

FORTNITE FACT

His tagline is 'a license to peel', in reference to the James Bond spy films.

B.R.U.T.E. GUNNER

Though not the rarest skin in this bunch, B.R.U.T.E. Gunner is definitely one of the slickest. The jet black bodysuit and matching helmet make her a nimble combatant, and hard to spot in the darker areas of the map.

FORTNITE FACT

She still appears in the shop every now and then, so save up your V-Bucks.

MIDAS

With a reactive feature that can turn weapons and vehicles gold, Midas is a glittering outfit with menacing characteristics. His gameplay-affecting ability makes him feared.

FORTNITE FACT

Collected at level 100 of the Battle Pass in Chapter 2, Season 2.

DREAM

This perky, purple pixie brings a certain sparkle to the island! She first fluttered into battle - and onto our list of faves - during Season 8 of Chapter 1.

FORTNITE FACT

Dream is available for 1200 V-Bucks when she's in the Item Shop.

MANCAKE

This skin is good enough to eat! Mancake - a living stack of pancakes with a butter bandalero - is a breakfast bandit that comes in selectable styles such as Lonesome Hero, Dark Deeds and the Cake With No Name.

FORTNITE FACT

Before Mancake, Agent Peely and Peely were the only other Battle Pass outfits made of food.

MALICE

This legendary skin is a hot-headed competitor with a devilish streak. Pair her with the Malice Wings back bling to increase the terror she instills in her competition as she drops onto the island below.

FORTNITE FACT

Malice is one of two skins in the Diabolical set, alongside the equally fiery Dominion.

ENVOY

She may be known as Envoy, but she has her own business to take care of - grabbing the victory royale. She arrived during the second season of Chapter 2 and her bright green hair made her stand out amongst the slew of agents that came out around the same time.

FORTNITE FACT

Like B.R.U.T.E. Gunner, Envoy is often in the shop for 800 V-Bucks.

LUMINOS

Appearing to channel some sort of ethereal light, Luminos is an epic skin suitable for any occasion. The unusual helmet protects the identity of the wearer, but the moon and star sigils adorning the robes suggest that it might not be of this world.

FORTNITE FACT

Luminos is part of the Interstellar set, which also contains the Lunar Light and Astral Axe items.

CHAPTER 2 SKINS

MENACE

This Roman-themed gladiator was found as a Character at the Colossal Coliseum, before becoming a much sought-after skin in the Season 5 Battle Pass. We loved the gold and purple armour plating style.

FORTNITE FACT

Menace was the first legendary skin in the Season 5 Battle Pass.

LEXA

Her awesome anime style makes Lexa stand out from the crowd - it almost looks like she's from a completely different game. She has three alternative styles and her warstrike look is also pretty slick!

FORTNITE FACT

You needed to complete 52 quests to unlock Lexa's warstrike skin!

AURA

She may seem like an ordinary woman, but Aura is a gold-clad treasure hunter with a mysterious side. What is she keeping in those pouches? What do those tattoos mean? Is the gold chain too chunky? All good questions in need of answers.

FORTNITE FACT

The winter hunter variant adds the warm long sleeves to Aura's outfit.

MAGNUS

There's no mistaking the long blond beard and horned helmet of the Viking Magnus. Does he have something to do with the mysterious Viking settlement atop a mountain to the east of Snobby Shores?

FORTNITE FACT

Magnus is part of the Norse set along with the Huntress skin.

RAVAGE

For fans of the Raven skin, Ravage was a welcome addition to the Fortnite wardrobe. It's a legendary skin that first appeared in Chapter 1, but frequently appears in the shop. It also comes with a free contrail - Dark Feathers!

FORTNITE FACT

There's a halloween variant Bone Ravage, which is part of the Skull Squad set.

KONDOR

Dark, dangerous and adept at causing mass destruction, standing in Kondor's path is not a good idea. This spirit of vengeance has five different styles to choose from, one of which is a terrifying cyborg variant.

FORTNITE FACT

Kondor's Zero Point style was unlocked at level 220 of the Season 5 Battle Pass.

MAVE

If you like outfits that change, then Mave is perfect. She comes in two styles - shieldbreaker is the one shown. But she can also have hair that turns into snakes, and a fish tail that appears when she's swimming!

FORTNITE FACT

Another of Mave's selectable styles is the warrior-like outfit called unstoppable.

RAZOR

Dropping into combat with her Fierce Cloudpuff back bling, Razor is a feared sight to competitiors on the Island. The bell on her neck is an odd choice though, and sure to garner some unneccessary attention ...

FORTNITE FACT

Razor comes from the Battle Breakers set, based on another Epic Games title.

MIX AND MATCH

Pairing the perfect outfit with ideal extras is not always easy. Here are some slick suggestions for teaming things up with these cool costumes.

AXERONI

EXTRA CHEESE GLIDER

TOMATO HEAD

BRITE BLIMP

RAINBOW SMASH

BRITE GUNNER

CUDDLE WRAP CAMO

CUDDLE CRUISER

RECON RANGER

6-CARAT CUTTER

SHINE PACK BLING

DIAMOND DIVA

SLURP WRAP (ON AR)

FROST BLADE

SHIVER

SKY STRIPE

STRIPE SLICER

RUBY

BUBBLE POPPER

BUBBLY BOMBS

BUBBLE BOMBER

AXE-OLOTL

ASSAULT BOMBER

RAPTOR

PARTY ANIMAL

JUGGUS BACK BLING

SLURP LEVIATHAN

CELESTIA

STARDUST STRIKERS

NUCLEUS

DRIVE TIME

Cars raced across the island's roads (and fields!) in Chapter 2. Gamers had long been keen for proper vehicles to make an entrance in Fortnite, and they weren't disappointed when they finally arrived.

TIP

Some radio stations can be played in the cars, so don't forget to check out the tunes while riding.

COOL CARS

At first there were four main types of cars in Battle Royale – the Mudflap truck, Whiplash sports car, Prevalent family wagon and OG Bear pickup truck. The machines arrived as part of the Joy Ride update.

ROAD RAGE

The motors move best when driven on the usual roads and solid surfaces. So if you want to put the pedal to the floor and reach serious speed, stick to the highways and concrete routes. However, the OG Bear copes with off-road grass and mud very well.

HIT THE GAS

Of course, these cars won't run and run … eventually they need refueling. A trip to the nearest gas station is then needed to keep you on the move. If you struggle to find one, keep a look out for small gas cans that appear around the island.

TYRE WEAR

Take care of the wheels, because after heavy driving and use the tyres can pop, leaving your car in a perilous driving condition. If your vehicle becomes too manic to control, ditch it and look for a fresh one to get behind the wheel of.

MEGA MATS

Remember that cars are a great source of materials too. If you run out of fuel or see a higher grade car you'd like to use instead, get your harvesting tool out and start bashing it up. You'll soon stock up a decent rate of metal.

TILTED TAXI

Just a few weeks after cars arrived, the fun and frantic Tilted Taxis LTM landed. The idea was to pick up and drop off certain passengers, collecting driver rating stars along the way. Plus, the taxi never ran out of fuel, so you weren't driven mad by the fuel gauge!

INCREDIBLE ITEMS

Chapter 2 delivered some awesome new items, from cool crystals to helpful healing tools and epic explosives. Dive in and explore the best of these fab features.

ITEM TYPE:
Foraged

ZERO POINT CRYSTALS

Discovered around the Zero Point in the desert biome of Season 5, break up the purple-pink crystals to earn a speedy reward. Consume them and then double jump and the user rockets forward in the direction they face. Effectively they act like a teleporting tool.

GOOD FOR:
Speeding away from dangerous situations.

ITEM TYPE:
Healing

ZERO POINT FISH

Also known as zero point flopper and located in several areas of water all over the map, these helpful fish heal 15 points. Plus, they can also grant a small level of the powers that a zero point crystal can provide. Well worth stacking.

GOOD FOR:
Reviving your health and getting a handy teleport to boot.

ITEM TYPE:
Healing

ITEM TYPE:
Healing

CHUG SPLASH

A rare throwable healing item, when chucked the chug splash will revive players or enemies within its short radius by 20 health and 20 shield. The item can be thrown a maximum of 18 floor tiles and be held in a stack of six.

TIP

The chug splash item can also be used to put out fires, although its healing powers are a much more effective use of the item, so don't waste it.

GOOD FOR:
Propping up your squad after taking some serious hits.

ITEM TYPE:
Healing

ITEM TYPE:
Explosive

FIREFLY JAR

An awesome addition to the game, the firefly jar and the fearsome fireflies inside unleash severe damage to players or buildings. When thrown, the jar deals 40 damage to an opponent on impact and can also set surrounding trees and wooden buildings aflame.

SHIELD FISH

Coming in lots of different colours, from deep blue to pink and pretty green stripes, shield fish can grant you a very decent 50 shield upon being fished by a player. These fish are found in a range of places, but remember that the famous pink fish needs a pro fishing rod to scoop it from the water.

GOOD FOR:
Boosting your strength in readiness to reach the mid and late game.

GOOD FOR:
Direct hits to an enemy in the late game and creating red-hot mayhem.

39

GAME-CHANGER: SHAKEDOWNS

In squad play, the shakedown option is a mighty weapon in helping to defeat the enemy team. Take a look at how this popular feature works in action.

WHAT IS A SHAKEDOWN?

When an opponent is knocked down, there's an opportunity to engage in a shakedown. This grabbing motion then reveals the locations of that player's nearby teammates, which can give your squad the upper hand in a tense team tussle and lead you straight to the remaining players.

E Shakedown

F Carry

WHEN DOES IT WORK?

The shakedown only works in squad games as its focus is on letting the 'shaker' know the whereabouts of rival fighters. The feature was first used in Season 2 of Chapter 2. Back then, it also revealed the location of local chests and items or helped lead you to hidden henchmen.

40

HOW CAN YOU SPOT THE ENEMY?

Performing a shakedown causes red markers to appear on the screen. These signal where your enemy is lurking, helping you and your squad to zone in and destroy them, because your fellow players will also see the marked spots. This gives your squad a big advantage.

ANY DISADVANTAGES TO A SHAKEDOWN?

If you're the person doing the shaking, then it's a great feature in helping you rack up eliminations. The only major downside to using it is that during a shakedown, you can be exposed to enemy fire. The shakedown lasts for a few seconds and can't be stopped, meaning you can't build or run to get away from attacks.

VAULTED & UNVAULTED

Keeping up to date with what's in and out of the game can be tricky. Here are some of the top things that have been vaulted and unvaulted during Chapter 2.

B.R.U.T.E. MECH

The poster-child for overpowered items, the B.R.U.T.E mech gives two players massive offensive and defensive potential. The driver has access to dash, stomp and jump attacks, while the passenger is shielded by a forcefield and is able to fire a shotgun cannon. Thankfully, it was vaulted in the first season of Chapter 2.

VAULTED

X-4 STORMWING

In Chapter 2, Season 5, the Operation Snowdown mission brought back the X-4 Stormwing to raise the winter wonderment of the game. With a cool Christmas look, the planes gave gamers a blast from the past. It was the first time a vehicle had been unvaulted and players flew in for a piece of the action! It can carry a whole squad of four, and the driver can use its guns.

UNVAULTED

TIP

When the X-4 Stormwing returned, it required fuel to keep it going, something that wasn't a feature in Chapter 1.

BANDAGE BAZOOKA

The bandage bazooka has been in and out of Fortnite more times than the Battle Bus! It seems strange that it first appeared at the start of Chapter 2, because it feels like it's been around for years, and this helpful squad healing tool has been vaulted and unvaulted several times through Chapter 2. When it's in play, make the most of its reviving powers, but remember it needs two inventory slots.

UNVAULTED

CHUG JUG

Surprisingly, the chug jug was vaulted from the main Battle Royale mode in Season 1 of Chapter 2, though it has since appeared in a couple of LTMs. It had the power to fully replenish health and shields over the course of 15 seconds, which makes it probably the most powerful healing item to ever hit the game. Many thought it was pretty balanced though!

VAULTED

TOP SECRET

LAUNCH PAD

Part of the game since the dawn of time (well, 2017), launch pads were finally unvaulted in the first season of Chapter 2 after they disappeared in the autumn of 2019. The pad boosts a player into the air, allowing glider redeploy and the ability to cover the map very easily. Sadly, they were vaulted again in Season 4 and available only in Creative.

VAULTED

JOIN THE PARTY!

Epic Games invited Fortnite fans to 'hop on the party bus' when Party Royale arrived in Chapter 2. Find out what this funky place is all about and the fun features it offers.

TIP

The BTS-inspired emotes, called I'm Diamond and It's Dynamite, were part of the BTS Dynamite Pack launched to celebrate the pop group's Party Royale entrance in Chapter 2.

WELCOME IN

Party Royale is a mode in Fortnite that's totally unlike the regulars of solo, duos and squad battles. For starters, there's no battling or building! You won't be eliminated in this area by a superior opponent, so just relax and enjoy things like special movie screens, music concerts and crazy minigames.

FREE TO PLAY

Like the rest of Fortnite Battle Royale, there's no charge to enter this social hangout and players enjoy hooking up with their buddies and taking it easy. The Big Screen is one of the most popular zones, found in the B4 and C4 area in the west central location.

THE BIG SCREEN

MAIN FOCUS

Don't confuse the Big Screen movie place with Party Royale's Main Stage, over in the east. Here, music superstars like BTS and Diplo have performed material during Chapter 2, with millions checking in on the concerts.

MINIGAMES

With no opponents to hunt down, Party Royale instead lets you explore some mega minigames and experience a different kind of victory compared to the main island. These will often follow a current theme within the game or link to a promoted feature, or could involve new Chapter 2 faves such as driving and swimming. Motorboats and quadcrashers were two of the earliest vehicles in Party Royale.

THE PLAZA

MAIN STAGE

RETURNING ITEMS

Keep an eye out for popular items popping up in Party Royale. Early on, favourites like the jetpack and the grappler featured, as well as exclusive stuff like the purple and orange paint launchers. These tame weapons only do minimal damage to vehicles and won't harm players – remember that Party Royale is a totally safe space.

SHARP STUFF

Party Royale is always ready to show off new and exciting features and content, so watch out for announcements from Epic about what's coming up. When it celebrated Shark Week on the Big Screen, players got a close-up look at one of the most fascinating and fearsome creatures on the planet ... even scarier than the mythic infinity blade!

EPIC EVENTS & LETHAL LTMs

Special events and Limited Time Mode (LTM) games have a huge appeal to Fortnite players of all abilities and experience. In Chapter 2, Battle Royalers have been treated to some top-class action.

SPY GAMES

One of the biggest events in Chapter 2 came in Season 2's sensational Spy Games. In fact, it was one of the biggest and most impactful storylines ever to appear in Battle Royale. Based around the Shadow and Ghost teams, players chose a side, took part in operations and fought to gain intel and unlock tech. Tech could be a variety of items, weapons or in-game benefits.

Upon reaching a new tier, new weapons and items were at your disposal, which could include the shield bubble, clinger and the exclusive creepin' cardboard. Powerful firearms, such as the tactical shotgun, heavy AR and bolt-action sniper could also be won. At the highest tier of 50, Midas' drum gun (Ghost) and TNTina's ka-boom bow (Shadow) were all yours.

Operation game modes included the Dropzone LTM, Payload, Infiltration and Knockout, and allowed a variety of team sizes. The best tech and tactics were needed to defeat teams and progress.

THE SPY WITHIN

Continuing with the spy theme, Season 5's The Spy Within mode was undoubtedly inspired by the huge PC and mobile game called *Among Us*. This became a mighty popular game at the end of 2020 and Epic devised its own spy-based take on the genre to appease its fans.

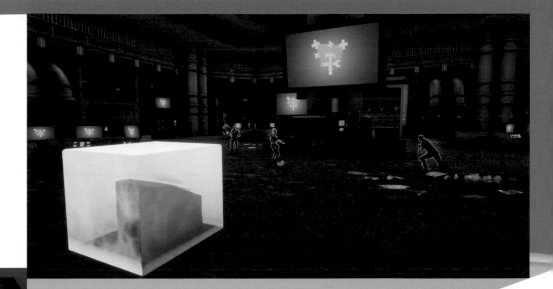

In The Spy Within, a team of agents had to identify the mysterious spies, gathering gold coins by finishing objectives and only communicating and discussing who the rogue players were through a meeting. New maps were routinely added to this mode and rewards were picked up, including the jingle wing glider and the wrapping caper back bling. Winners were determined by completing tasks or by the spies being discovered.

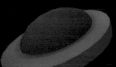

EPIC EVENTS & LETHAL LTMs

FOG OF WAR

This is perfect for the sneaky spies that have been descending on the island for most of Season 2. There's a thick fog across the whole of the island, which means snipers are out and supressed weapons are in.

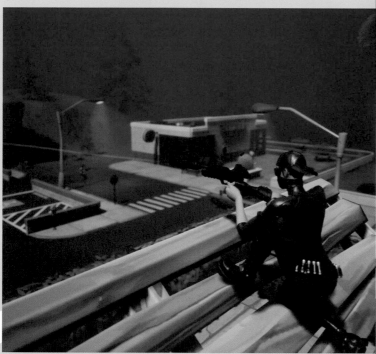

You'll be able to crouch and sneak faster in this LTM, which adds to the espionage. When you eliminate a player, you'll restore either your health or your shield. Even if you don't knock a player down, you'll still reveal their position on the map so you can chase them down!

Islanders may know this game mode by a different name - Sneaky Silencers - which was what it was called when it was first released in January 2018. Some weapons available have changed since the first incarnation, however.

MARVEL-LOUS MATCHES

For the last couple of years, Marvel has had some mind-blowing linkups with Fortnite. Aside from classic outfits like Deadpool, Black Widow and Star-Lord, Marvel-themed LTMs are among the most revered selection of limited game choices.

Marvel Takeover, in Chapter 2, Season 4, brought titanic team fights in a raging super storm. Involving Galactus and the moving storm shield, your adventure began with being handed a random superpower.

Marvel fans also lapped up the Marvel Venom Cup in Chapter 2, which was part of the Marvel Super Series that finished with a $1 million prize pool Super Cup event. Broadcast live on the Fortnite YouTube and Twitch channels, Super Cup was a prestigious event, requiring players to have an account with at least level 30.

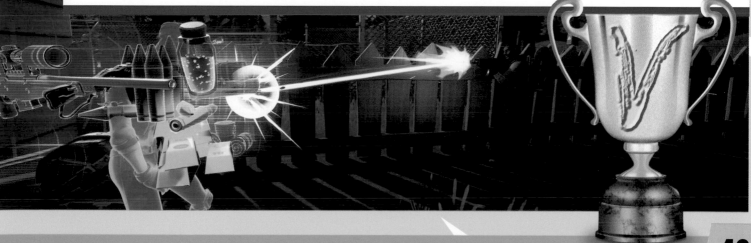

10 TOP TACTICS

Taking down the opposition is a serious business, requiring slick moves and techniques to get the upper hand. Follow these tactics, tips and ideas to become an ace eliminator around the island.

1

KNOW NEW MOVES

Fortnite's mechanics and special features get updated and improved all the time. New moves and details are added each season, with even grander developments brought in at the start of a new Chapter. In Chapter 2, Season 5, the sand around the Zero Point could be used to your advantage, if you knew how to make your stand ...

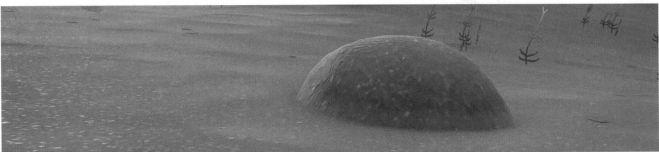

Standing still on the sand made you slowly sink. No need to worry, though, as no damage was done to your health. Once hidden under the golden grains, you could move with increased speed and not be seen by others, apart from a small moving mound above you. Enemies could fire at you if they spotted the moving sand, which would eventually force you to reappear above the surface.

2 CRYSTAL CLEAR

The zero point crystals were revealed on page 38, but here's more helpful intel on how to exploit them. The crystals appeared in Chapter 2 of Season 5, and the top gamers soon started using them to reach opponents lurking on high ground, instead of having to ramp up with builds. Making your character look up and then using this boost flings you upwards – no need to use mats and build. These cool crystals really were a game-changer.

3 TACTICAL TIME

The tactical shotgun was vaulted in Season 4, but soon returned in the following season, complete with a power boost. If firing accuracy is one of your weaknesses, keep this weapon at the ready because it can compensate hugely with its impressive spread and high fire rate. At close range it can be ultra effective and remember it has a mag size of eight, compared to five for the pump shotgun. Reload time is its downside, though.

10 TOP TACTICS

4 FISH FORCE

The ability to fish was only introduced in Chapter 2, and by Season 5, there were over 40 types of fish to find in the waters. Many offer healing benefits, which are always welcome, but the five types of rift fish added something new entirely. Coming in volcanic, butterfly, black spotted, sandstorm and galactic types (the last two require a pro rod) they had the ability to spawn a rift and allow players to quickly zoom through the sky – great tactic to escape battles and cover ground.

5 DRIVE & REVIVE

Cruising around in a car in Chapter 2 is cool, but remember that while you're in the driver's seat you can't take on meds. Swap to the passenger's seat (the car will keep rolling for a short while) revive yourself and then hop back behind the wheel. Passengers are also able to fire weapons in the car, so make sure your teammates are locked and loaded while you're driving with your mates.

6 KEEP THE LINE

Even with the new mechanics and features in Chapter 2, keeping control of your line of sight should never be far from your mind. This refers to your vision over what's in front of you, or more specifically, the sight line you have through to your enemy target. Taking a high spot on a building or structure you create often improves your line of sight. You need 'eyes on the prize' but also try to stay out of range of your opponent.

7 LOADOUT STRATEGY

Having the right 'stuff' in your five slots is still as relevant now in Chapter 2 as it was back in the day. Your loadout strategy will be based around your own preferences, ability and combat style. As a general rule, three weapons are often placed in slots one, two and three, with at least one healing item in the other slots. Explosives are also popular. Typically, many pros opt for a shotgun, SMG and AR as their weapons, in that order.

TIP

Try arranging weapons in order of their effectiveness. So, shotties are in slot one because they are for close range, then comes the submachine gun, followed by the distance-focused rifle.

10 TOP TACTICS

TIP

Try to learn quickly where vehicles and boats spawn around the island. Having this detailed knowledge could be a lifeline.

8

STAY MOBILE

You gotta keep quick on your feet, especially early on! Moving around to harvest mats and weapons is essential after you drop. If you don't, opponents will soon send you to your knees. Chapter 2 has seen cars and boats enter the island, so use these to get across the land quickly if you need to.

Dropping in remote areas is preferred by lots of gamers – it affords you time to explore the surroundings without constant fear of attacks. But, these quiet zones may force you to move fast when the storm whips up, so always be ready to rock and travel on in your quest to survive.

LEARN TO LOVE LTMS

There is always a limited time mode (LTM) to take part in, from huge team rumbles to new themes and action-based adventures. Never write these off as a waste of time. Taking part in LTMs can really boost your skills, giving you new tools and tactics to adopt when you're back in a regular Battle Royale. LTMs often allow you to respawn, which means you can get back into the game quickly and practise more vital techniques. So stay up to date with what special events you can join.

FIGHT V BUILD

Knowing the best time to fight and the best time to build is not really something you can be taught. With more Battle Royale experience and game time, your abilities will increase and your instincts around the 'fight versus build' option will develop naturally. Slapping down a big ol' structure and using up key mats is a waste when an accurate headshot could just do the job much more quickly and easy.

GET COMPETITIVE

Taking your game powers to the next level needs lots of hard work, practice and some serious skill. Here, you'll discover some of the top competitive tournaments of recent times, and what's needed to succeed with the best of the best!

FORTNITE CHAMPION SERIES

The OG Fortnite Champion Series, known as FNCS, kicked off in Season X (remember that far back?!) and was unique at the time because it was a trio-based tournament for players who really wanted a tough test. It has remained an online-only trio team competition throughout 2021, with players who rank as champion division in Arena able to take part. It takes proper organised team play to work through this tense tournament.

DREAMHACK

In 2020, DreamHack was firmly established as a hot monthly tournament to follow on streaming sites such as Twitch. As a deadly duos format, it follows a structure of two open stages, with the top 250 from each progressing to the semis. From there, the 50 finest pairs are involved in the final. With strong competitors from North America and Europe, there's no point getting involved unless you have stacks of serious skills on the island!

FRIDAY NITE BRAGGING RIGHTS

Want to set yourself up nicely for the weekend? Launched in January 2021, Friday Nite Bragging Rights gives your trio of mates that perfect way to celebrate across Saturday and Sunday. Divided into PC, console and mobile divisions, this competitive regional contest earned successful players a sick shout out from the @FNCompetitive account!

ARENA ACTION

Playing in the Arena game mode is a load of hype ... literally! This highly competitive setting, accessed through the tab in the lobby, rewards Hype points to players as they earn eliminations, Victory Royales and other achievements. The highest Hype earners are given the chance to take part in online events, earn rewards and even be part of cash-based competitions.

CREATE YOUR ISLAND

Fortnite Creative appeared during Christmas 2018. Over the years, gamers have continued to explore this imaginative place, where cool tools are used to create your own games and experiences for the community to enjoy. Turn over for some awesome codes to enter, but first, here is a mini guide to this clever feature ...

CREATIVE
SELECT A SERVER

ISLAND CODE

CREATE
Create your own unique games and play with your friends!
LAUNCH

PLAY

ESC **CANCEL**

HOW TO ENTER

Select the type of island you want to build on, such as arctic, temperate or meadow, and name it. You can begin adding prefab buildings, devices, weapons and consumables to the island and start creating minigames for the people you invite. Remember that Creative is not like Battle Royale – its focus is on making your own structures, features, rules and games.

RIFTS

From the Creative Hub, there are plenty of places displayed for you to visit by entering the rifts in front of you. These can be from Epic and community creators. You can spend hours entering new and exciting zones and picking up ideas and tips of what to place down in your own map. Learn from these experienced Creative dudes!

ENCEPHALON

STORM

CUSTOMISE

Your AR phone is a key piece of kit when building and creating. It allows you to move and place objects that you've selected from the menu, so that buildings, cars and devices are in the spot that you want and interact with each other exactly how you intend them to.

GAMES GALORE

From adventure, survival, prop hunt and puzzle, to escape mazes, deathrun and parkour, there are so many types of games to jump in on and put a smile on your face. When you've had enough of tense Battle Royales, go to Creative mode for a different slice of Fortnite fun.

PRACTICE

Yes, Creative can be an awesome place to practise and sharpen your skills, from building to one-on-ones and weapon handling. Play around with the settings, go crazy with the 'fly around' option to look at your builds from all angles and play within the limits that you place on yourself. Let your imagination rule!

CREATIVE CODES

There are thousands of codes in the Creative world, letting you pick and play the best offerings from the creator community. Epic often releases its favourite codes and likes to back up and coming creators in the hub. Here are some of the hottest codes and maps to explore.

BHE 1V1 BUILD FIGHTS 8064-7152-2934

Mastered by Fortnite Creative expert BHE, who comes from Egypt, Epic gave big shout outs to this creator over the last couple of years. His one-on-one map has been a huge draw, allowing players to perfect their combat skills in close-quarter scraps. Hone your box-fighting abilities in this popular island too.

CLIX BOX FIGHTS 7620-0771-9529

Box fighting obviously happens in a very small, restricted space. It's similar to a build fight, and lots of Creative folk refer to it as the 'meta' of Fortnite – meaning it's the ultimate goal and shows your superiority. Check out Clix Box Fights island and get boasting about your boxing abilities.

SNIPER ONE SHOT 6103-8566-5742

This Creative space is the perfect place to settle a grudge, or just work out once and for all who the best shot is. Players will drop from one of the towers into a vast open area, equipped with a legendary sniper rifle. The only purpose is to take out anyone else in the arena with you and rack up the eliminations. Winners here will be those with a steady hand and an eagle eye.

50 LEVEL DEFAULT DEATHRUN 3612-4233-8481

If you've got a need for speed, then this parkour game is perfect. Up to 16 players can take on the 50 levels of this assault course in order to see who's the fastest. It starts off super simple – some easy jumps will be enough to get you through the first levels. The difficulty ramps up with electrified obstacles and spike traps littering later levels. Your progress is saved at each checkpoint in case you die.

STRAY KITE FARMS 6069-9263-9110

Billed as both a prop hunt and hide-and-seek style minigame, Stray Kite Farms challenges 16 players to take control of the seemingly peaceful landscape by morphing into objects. It's a team-based trial, with two rounds played before the roles are reversed and the game switches up. This particular game is made by StrayKite, the brains behind popular Creative minigames such as Prop Heist and Stray Kite Docks.

CYBERNITE 2 5959-5776-7711

Jumping on the cyberpunk bandwagon that rolled through 2020, Cybernite 2 is a delightfully futuristic showcase created by jesse-ocegueda. It's a neon-infused platforming adventure, where you take on the role of a hacker, tasked with gaining secrets from a shady corporation and avoiding its lackeys, who will try to stop you. It's a stylish sequel that shows how much you can achieve in Creative.

CREATIVE CODES

SPY WITHIN 0288-3600-7090

Most island games accommodate up to 16 players, but Spy Within is for between five to ten, just like the *Among Us* PC and mobile game it is based on. As a group, the crew must seek out and identify an impostor hiding in their midst. If they can't work out who it is then there's a good chance that the whole group will be wiped out. Get your magnifying glass ready!

RUPTURE 5065-7222-5327

Searching for enemies to shoot in Fortnite can be time-consuming, but you'll never have that problem in Rupture. Enemy hordes will flock to you in a neon-lit town and you can mow down crowds at a time. The more you defeat, the more coins you'll earn, which you can use to unlock buildings and discover caches of even better weapons and items.

HONEYCOMB HEIGHTS 3428-2420-5841

Creative can be a weaponsfest if you choose, and Honeycomb Heights carries the tagline 'gun game' for good reason! This PvP free-for-all is packed to the brim with action, with busy settings providing the base for player eliminations and the chance to pick up higher grade weapons. With points and voting a big function, there's plenty going on all the time.

LLAMA LEAGUE 5065-8745-9382

If you've played *Rocket League*, then Llama League is right up your racetrack! It's a four-player team-based mini game, with the blue cars revving up against reds in one of five special arenas. The objective is to score five goals from within your vehicles, with a round-based strategy determining the champions. It's perfect for practising car handling.

RTX SURVIVE THE NIGHT CHALLENGE 5511-7018-2692

Ray tracing (known as RTX) came to Fortnite on PC in the early autumn of 2020. It's just a fancy tech word for enhanced visual or lighting effects. RTX Survive the Night makes full use of the graphic-sharpening technology in this beautiful mode, which challenges solos, doubles or trios to battle through 30 fearsome waves of deadly monsters that have risen from the grave and stalk the night. Enter the code now ... if you're brave enough!

FIRE & ICE GUN FRIGHT 6178-3809-0428

Medieval warriors? Tick. Gun fights? Tick. Dragons? Tick! Creator Ducc delivers all these weird and wonderful elements, plus a whole load more, in this epic survival game that came to Creative during Season 5. Players are assigned to either team fire or team ice and given a random loadout before being released onto the feudal-style map. If the many passages, tunnels and outposts weren't enough, it also has its own storm circle!

BATTLE ROYALE BRAIN BUSTERS

How many Fortnite facts, stats and pieces of info do you have stored in your head? Take the quiz over the next four pages to find out what level of know-how you really have.

1 What was the name of the update that brought cars to the island?

....

2 Which location appeared in E6, near Weeping Woods and Lazy Lake, in Chapter 2, Season 5?

....

3 What does FNCS stand for in competitive play?

....

4 What's the name of this Character from Chapter 2?

....

5 By how much HP can a cabbage heal?

....

6 How many V-Bucks does the Battle Pass cost?

....

7 Flapjack Flyer, Razor Crest and Hyperboard are all types of what?

....

8 What mode did Battle Lab replace in Chapter 2?

....

13 What does POI mean around the map?

....

9 The Big Screen and Main Stage are found in what mode?

....

14 What has the largest magazine size – heavy assault rifle, tactical shotgun or bolt-action sniper rifle?

....

10 What's the name of the app Fortnite launched new quiz content on in Chapter 2?

....

15 This is the outline of which popular outfit?

....

11 What fuel-powered backpack item, vaulted in Chapter 2, could fly players around for a limited time?

....

12 What type of bullets does this symbol represent?

....

16 True or false? Fortography is Epic's campaign to promote the best community-made gameplay images.

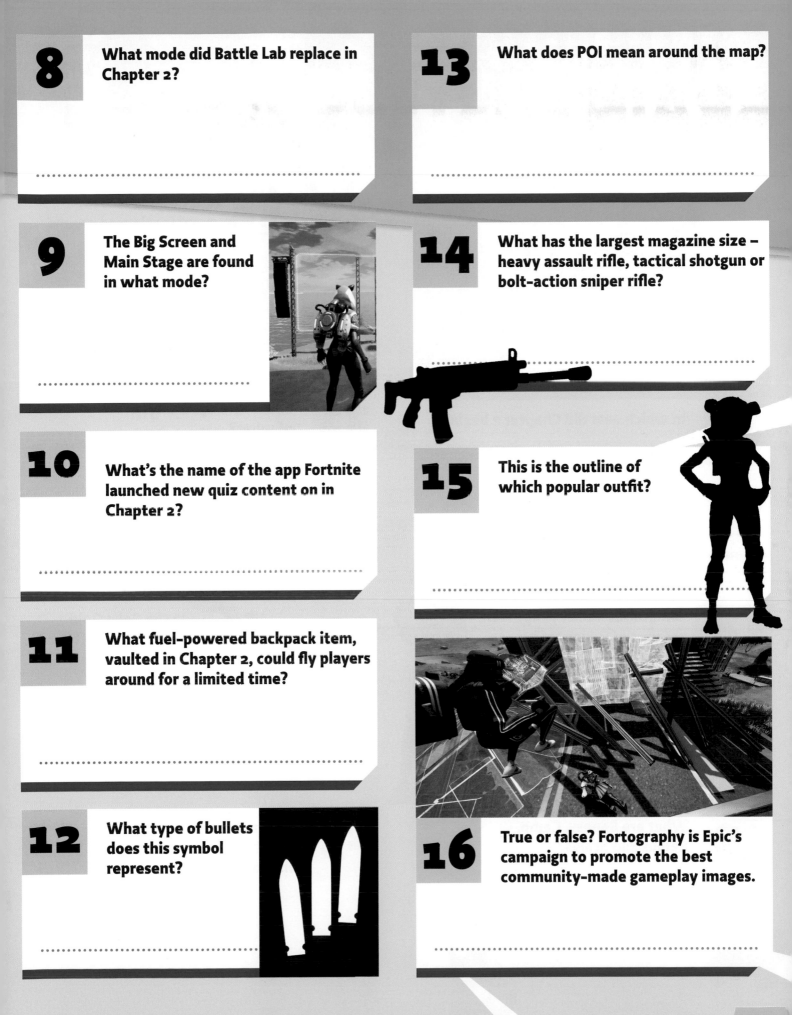

BATTLE ROYALE BRAIN BUSTERS

17
In which year did Chapter 2 begin?

18
Tomatohead and PJ Pepperoni are part of which set?

19
What are Bonesy, Camo, Remus and Scales?

20
What famous seasonal event is released around Halloween?

21
Shells 'n' slugs is a type of what?

22
In the Solid Gold LTM, what rarity are all the weapons?

23
How many players could ride in the shopping cart?

24
What type of fishing rod has a small Peely attached to the end?

....

27
In which season were gold bars and bounties introduced?

....

25
Identify three locations or POIs that have the initials SS.

....

28
What was the first mythic weapon added to Battle Royale?

....

29
Malice is one of the two skins available in the Diabolical set. What's the name of the other one?

....

26
How many digits are in a Creative island code?

....

30
Can you name the non-drivable vehicle that works with a reboot card to revive a team-mate?

....

Answers: 1. Joy Ride update; **2.** Hunter's Haven; **3.** Fortnite Champion Series; **4.** Mancake; **5.** 10 HP; **6.** 950; **7.** Glider; **8.** Playground; **9.** Party Royale; **10.** House Party; **11.** Jetpack; **12.** Medium bullets; **13.** Point of interest; **14.** Heavy assault rifle; **15.** Cuddle Team Leader; **16.** True; **17.** 2019; **18.** Pizza Pit; **19.** Pets; **20.** Fortnitemares; **21.** Bullet/ammunition; **22.** Legendary; **23.** Two; **24.** Pro fishing rod; **25.** Slurpy Swamp, Steamy Stacks, Sweaty Sands, Stealthy Stronghold, Salty Springs, Shifty Shafts, Snobby Shores, Starry Suburbs, Sunny Steps; **26.** 12; **27.** Chapter 2, Season 5; **28.** Infinity blade; **29.** Dominion; **30.** Reboot van

BACK LATER, FOLKS!

This might be where our journey finishes, but in Fortnite the adventure never ends. The game changes every season, bringing new themes, weapons and surprises. It's why we love it so much, and why a Victory Royale remains as sweet now as back in 2018.

Fortnite promises to evolve, improve and cement its position as the world's ultimate videogame in 2022. We can look forward to amazing additions, new challenges, lethal LTMs and top-class competitive play. Events like the Fortnite World Cup, Party Royale streams and epic Creative builds will take us all to the next level.

So warm up for your solo showdown or call on your squad for another attack on the island, because it's time to board the Battle Bus and drop in on the never-ending adventure.